# Cleanliness is next to...

# Cleanliness is next to...

**Life's
most
essential
cleaning
tasks**

**Stewart, Tabori & Chang · New York**

Published by
Stewart, Tabori & Chang
A Company of La Martinière Groupe
115 West 18th Street
New York, NY 10011

Export Sales to all countries except Canada, France,
and French-speaking Switzerland:
Thames and Hudson Ltd.
181A High Holborn
London WC1V 7QX
England

Canadian Distribution:
Canadian Manda Group
One Atlantic Avenue, Suite 105
Toronto, Ontario M6K 3E7
Canada

Library of Congress Cataloging-in-Publication Data

Taylor, Clarice.
        Cleanliness is next to... : life's most essential cleaning tasks / by Clarice Taylor.
            p. cm.
        ISBN 1-58479-350-3
        1. House cleaning. I. Title.

TX324.T39 2004
648'.5–dc22

                                                                        2003066803

Printed in China

10 9 8 7 6 5 4 3 2 1

First Printing

**To Zi with love, for all your help and encouragement.**

*Cleanliness is next to...* would not have been if not for the supportive Leslie Stoker, creative Larissa Nowicki and team at STC—the visionary Marisa Bulzone, wonderfully conscientious Elaine Schiebel. Thanks Marisa for the idea and to the others for its brilliant form. Thank you Toni Barton for your divine photography and styling skills. You were like a blessed angel sent from heaven.

# Introduction

**Philosophers from Aristotle and Nietzsche to Stevie Wonder have extolled the virtue of cleanliness.** The latter sang, "her clothes are old, but never are they dirty," a testament to the character of a poor but honorable family. Be it grand or ever so humble, a clean, well-ordered environment can be a refuge from modern, hectic life.

A little care—and of the right kind—will enhance and preserve the items in your physical environment. Cleaning and upkeep don't have to take a lot of time, money, and expertise. In these pages you will find tried and true cleaning techniques that save time and money.

Many of the cleaners you need are already in your home. Alka Seltzer is great for cleaning jewelry. Plain white toothpaste is effective on water rings on wood furniture. Your home may already be a treasure trove of cleaning and polishing agents.

While some cleaning projects are best left to professionals, there is plenty you can do yourself, with great results. One of my fondest memories is of my father polishing our shoes on Saturday night in preparation for church the next day. He had built his own shoeshine box and stocked it with quality brushes and polishes in all the right colors. We kids never tired of watching him; it seemed an act of love. Our Sunday-morning best owed much to Dad's spit shine, which made our shoes gleam and kept them looking like new.

*Cleanliness is next to...,* seasoned with wisdom, love, and humor, is a quiet celebration of values that are being lost in the rush of modern life. Hectic lives mean we seldom experience the spiritual and emotional satisfaction of standing back and taking in the freshness of something newly cleaned.

Newlyweds, new parents, students, and busy professionals will all find techniques in this little book to help them keep their belongings and treasures clean.

# Essential Cleaning Arsenal: What to Keep on Hand

# Acquiring possessions is part of life

Some are purely practical; others are valued treasures. Proper care is the key to maintaining them and ensuring their longevity.

Many of the techniques in this book are based on care and cleaning agents that are already in your home. Using these household items on a regular basis will yield surprising results.

Once, on a flight home from a late meeting in Washington in the spring, I had been served a glass of red wine when the plane lurched and the wine became one with my beautiful coat. The flight attendant had covered this territory before. She brought several cans of club soda and a mound of white towels. I placed several towels under the coat and daubed it with others soaked in club soda. The would-be stain began to lift immediately. By the time we landed, my coat was stain-free.

Having witnessed that demonstration of its power, I rarely drink club soda anymore. But I acquired a profound respect for around-the-house cleaning agents.

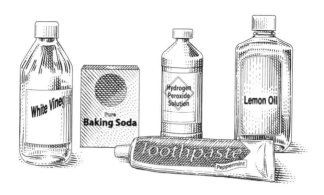

**Some of the champions are already in your medicine or kitchen cabinets:**

White Vinegar, Baking Soda, Hydrogen Peroxide, Lemon or Lemon Oil, White Toothpaste, Salt, Cornstarch, Alka Seltzer, Rubbing Alcohol, Cream of Tartar, and Denture Cleaning Tablets.

All are great cleaners. Keep them on hand. As stand-alones or in combination, they do the work of many commercial products at a fraction of the cost.

*You don't get anything clean*
*without getting something else dirty.*

CECIL BAXTER

**Warning:** Never mix bleach and ammonia.
The chemical reaction is potentially dangerous.

**No cleaning arsenal would be complete without:**

Bleach, ammonia, Murphy's oil soap, saddle soap

**These cleaning supplies are a must:**

Clean, soft cloths, cotton swabs, cotton squares, toothbrush

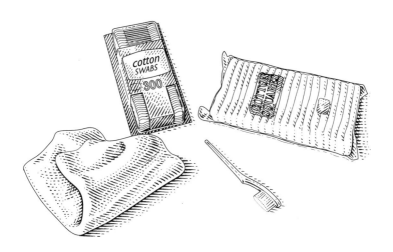

# Care and Cleaning of Common Household Items

**Basic Cleaning Terms:**

**Blot** A dabbing motion that absorbs moisture

**Buff** A back-and-forth motion with a cloth that polishes or burnishes

**Soft cloth** A cloth, preferably made of cotton, that contains no stiff or rough fibers

**Damp cloth** As much moisture as possible has been squeezed or wrung out by hand

**Wet cloth** Has been immersed in and is holding water, but is not saturated to the point of dripping

*Cleanliness and order are not matters of instinct;*
*they are matters of cultivation,*
*and like most great things,*
*you must cultivate a taste for them.*

BENJAMIN DISRAELI

**The key to preserving your possessions is preventive maintenance. Regular upkeep is essential.** This is not easy given today's lifestyles, but put yourself on a seasonal schedule for specific items. For example, clean upholstery at every seasonal solstice. Your belongings will stay clean and well maintained.

Treat stains and spots immediately, before they set. Have an emergency kit on hand with club soda, salt, vinegar, and hydrogen peroxide. Stock it with cotton swabs, cotton squares, and clean, soft cloths. When disaster strikes, you will be prepared.

When it comes to maintenance, in addition to reading and following instructions when you first purchase items, it is a good idea to keep any special instructions in a file for special reference. Correct storage is the key to maintenance. It is a good idea to save containers, such as shoe boxes, that also protect items once they are home.

Pay a bit more for excellent cleaning and maintenance service to prolong your investment in household goods and items you treasure.

Generic is not always a bargain. Keep that in mind when purchasing cleaning products. When not using homemade products, I have often found in the case of name brands that they have gotten items cleaner more quickly, saving repeat applications and in the long run, saving time and money.

Aerosol or the pump? When there is a choice, I choose the pump when purchasing household cleaning products. This is not entirely altruistic on my part. I am concerned about saving the environment, but I am also interested in saving time, money, and frustration. We have all experienced aerosol failure before the can was empty. It is also possible with a pump, to open the product and pour out a bit if you need a concentrated application.

# Life's Most Essential Cleaning Tasks

# Everything gets dirty

It's a fact of life. Accepting that can make the difference between seeing cleaning as drudgery or one of the vital activities of life. Keeping your home and valuables clean can be just as enjoyable as other, more highly regarded, household tasks such as cooking or sewing.

**1**

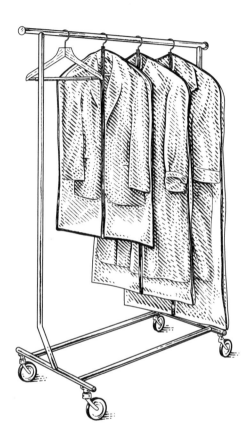

## Apparel

No wire hangers! Wooden and padded hangers are my favorites because they have roomy shoulders that support garments without stretching them. Keep the shoulders and arms of suit jackets and coats in shape by stuffing them with tissue paper. Only use white, since colored paper can run.

Keep air circulating where you store your clothing. That musty smell when you open your closet door can be eliminated by simply leaving the door ajar, even if it means disregarding that voice in your head that repeats Grandma's admonitions to always keep closet doors closed.

**Suits and Coats** Dry clean less frequently to prolong the life of your best suits and coats. Exposure to cleaning chemicals eventually damages fabrics and dulls colors.

Wear a suit a half dozen times before having it cleaned, and let the suit air out for about an hour before hanging it in your closet. An overcoat can be worn for a season before cleaning. Let suits and coats air out a day or two between wearings.

*Pearl of Preservation: Minimize the effect of chemical dry cleaning by removing your suits and coats from plastic dry cleaners bags as soon as possible and placing them in breathable cloth garment bags. If your newly dry-cleaned clothing smells heavily of chemicals when you pick them up, find another dry cleaner! Or invest in a linen garment bag for use in picking up your dry cleaning. You save the environment and lessen the effect of the cleaning chemicals on your clothing.*

**Sweaters, Lingerie, and Other Fine Washables** Gentle handling brings rewards. With patience and a gentle touch, wool and cashmere sweaters can be kept beautiful by handwashing. The key is to wash them often enough to keep dirt and odors from setting but not so often that they get stretched out.

Fill a basin with cold water and add a capful of your favorite delicate cleaner or baby shampoo. Be as gentle with your sweaters as you are with your hair.

Soak items one at a time for about three minutes, squeezing suds through the garment. Rinse by dipping garments in clean, cool water until there are no more suds. This will require draining and filling the sink several times. For extra freshness, add rose water or eau de cologne to the final rinse water.

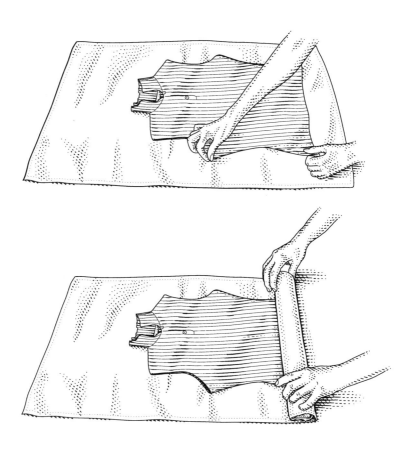

Prevent permanent stretching by rolling delicate items in a clean towel to remove excess water. Squeeze. Never twist or ring out. Lay flat on a fresh towel or mesh drying rack, and carefully reshape sweaters to their original size. For lingerie, no reshaping is necessary. Let air-dry away from heat or direct sunlight.

When you are too busy to handwash, care for wool and cashmere sweaters via a tag-team effort: alternate dry cleaning with handwashing. Handwash your sweaters at least once for every time sweaters are professionally cleaned.

✚ **Rescue:** *If you shrink your favorite wool or cashmere sweater, immerse it for a few minutes in a mixture of $\frac{1}{4}$ cup of hair conditioner to a gallon of cool water. Work the mixture through the sweater, gently but firmly. Avoid stretching. Do not ring it out. Roll the sweater in a clean, thick towel to absorb most of the water. Lay the sweater flat on a clean, dry towel or mesh drying rack. Gently pull the garment back to its original size.*

**2**

## Leather and Suede

Leather furniture is low maintenance as well as beautiful. But low does not mean no maintenance. As with all things, proper care is the key to preserving your leather furnishings. Stainproof by using a leather polishing agent suggested by the manufacturer (test an inconspicuous area first). Be sure to give special attention to areas that get extra wear. It is a good idea to clean and recondition your sofa or chair every six months.

**Leather Upholstery** Generally, leather upholstery can be cleaned simply with saddle soap. Readily available where leather is sold including shoe repair shops, saddle soap is an oil-based soap that comes in a paste and should be applied with a clean, damp (not saturated) cloth. Use gentle strokes to avoid stretching the leather. Blot any area where moisture is visible and let air-dry. Never use heat. When dry, increase the leather's suppleness and prevent tears by rubbing the hide with a soft cloth on which a bit of olive oil has been sprinkled, not poured.

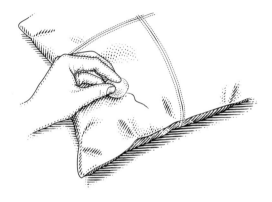

✚ **Rescue:** *Remove ink by dampening a clean cloth or cotton ball with hairspray or rubbing alcohol. Test an inconspicuous area for color fastness first. Dab the spot until the ink fades.*

**Suede Upholstery** With the exception of quick touch-ups, suede is always best cleaned by a professional. Bring in a professional once a year for a thorough cleaning and reapplication of water- and stain-guard agents.

For maintenance, stroke suede lightly in one direction (not back and forth) using a suede brush to remove dirt. Suede brushes come in various styles, but they all have short, wire bristles that raise pile and restore the surface texture. Done once a week, this simple technique will prolong the life and beauty of your suede upholstery.

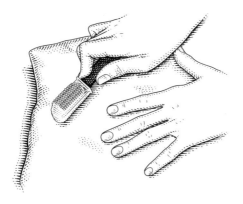

➕ **Rescue:** *A rubber cement pick-up, a small eraser-like object used to wipe off excess glue, available at art supply stores, is great for removing dirt spots from suede without ruining the pile.*

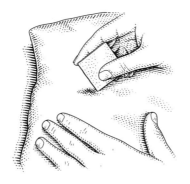

**Shoes and Boots** Preventive as well as regular maintenance extend the life of shoes and boots. Keep the box your shoes come in for storage and protection. Punch holes in the sides for air circulation and store in a cool, dry place away from leather-damaging humidity. If you don't have the original boxes, rather than store your shoes in plastic, which traps air and odors, use hanging bags made of canvas. The original stuffing will help shoes keep their shape, or better yet, shoe trees—wood or plastic—are a great investment.

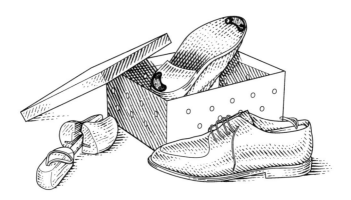

⧖ *Pearl of Preservation: Take new shoes to a shoe repair shop you trust right away and have toe and heel guards put on. For comfort as well as protection, have a thin rubber tread added underneath the ball of each sole. Shield the surface of suede and nonleather shoes with a coat of protective spray.*

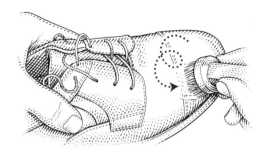

**Polish like a pro** For leather shoes, regular cleaning and polish will keep them functioning and looking great for a long time. Here's how: Wipe off dust and dirt with a soft cloth. Dampen (don't wet) a corner of the cloth with a one-to-one mixture of water and vinegar to remove any tough spots. Next, place shoes on shoetrees or stuff them with paper.

Use the best quality polish you can afford in a closely matching color. Keep neutral polish on hand for times when you need to replenish your stock but your shoes won't wait. Neutral polish is also best for shoes that have contrasting stitching.

Apply polish in a circular motion with a round polish brush made for the purpose of creating a pattern of swirls. In a pinch you can also use a cloth, but a brush puts more polish on the shoes. Once you have applied it, go back with a clean, lint-free cloth and begin to buff vigorously across the top of the shoe, moving on to the sides and back. Be energetic! In polishing shoes, as in life, you truly reap what you sow.

Devotees of the "spit shine," like my dad, say there is no substitute. If you choose to take your shoe shining up a notch, know that a little saliva once or twice between buffs goes a long way and yields a fabulous, professional-looking shine.

**Handbags and Briefcases** Polish leather handbags and briefcases as you would shoes and boots, and on a regular basis to keep them in good condition. You may need to use a toothbrush to clean the crevices, pockets and pouches.

Before polishing soft bags, stuff them with tissue or towels for a smooth surface. Apply neutral polish with a clean cloth and let stand for one hour. Buff with a clean, lint-free cloth. Be careful to remove all the polish if you are using black, brown, or other colors that can rub onto your clothes.

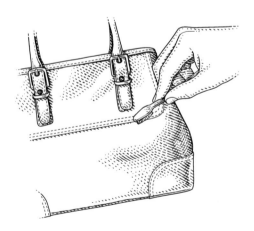

**Rescue:** *If your bag is scratched, fill in the mark with a color stick, available in hardware stores for use on scratched tables and floors, before polishing.*

Faded leather bags are best professionally redyed. Silk, canvas, or other cloth bags are best cleaned by professionals.

White vinegar, that household staple, works well on patent leather. Apply it to a clean soft cloth, rub the surface, and wipe off.

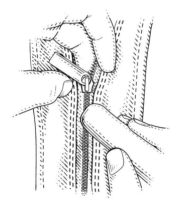

**Rescue:** *Unstick a stuck zipper on handbags or briefcases, whether it is open or closed, by rubbing the teeth with a candlestick or a bar of soap. Be careful to keep the soap away from the fabric of bags made of delicate material.*

# 3

## Wood Floors and Furniture

Treat wood like a living thing—well almost. Nothing adds beauty to your home like well cared–for, gleaming wood floors and furniture. There are many products on the market, but be sure to avoid those that are silicone-based, as they trap dirt and do not allow the wood to breathe. Whatever you use, avoid aerosol-based dusting products. They are quick, but in the long run, they are bad for the wood, toxic for you and your family, and destructive to the environment.

**Hardwood Floors** Sweep, dust mop, and vacuum wood floors weekly to keep them beautiful. Weekly damp-mopping in high-traffic areas or if you live in an area with high levels of air pollution, will prolong and enhance their beauty.

One homemade care regimen is to damp-mop frequently with a mixture of $\frac{1}{2}$ cup of vinegar to 1 gallon of water. Dip your mop into the solution. Wring out the mop well. Clean small sections of the floor, and dry with an old bath towel, keep water from soaking the floor. Change the solution frequently. Do not use dirty solution; once the water loses its clarity, it's time to change it.

Getting out the dirt while preserving the finish: For more intense cleaning, Murphy's Oil Soap is a traditional favorite. Follow the manufacturer's instructions.

Always avoid harsh detergents on wood floors.

✪ **Rescue:** *Cover scratches in wood floors with very fine steel wool dipped in floor wax or fill in the scratch with a color stick, available in hardware stores for use on scratched tables and floors. A mixture of floor polish and brown shoe polish will cover faded spots. A regular pencil eraser or kerosene takes out heel marks.*

**Wood Furniture** Regular dusting is essential to preserving and increasing the beauty of wood furniture. It is as important as washing a car before polishing it. Use a clean, soft, lint-free cloth. A soft toothbrush works well on ornately carved areas. The key to dusting is to go with, not against, the grain of the wood. Yogi Berra said, "You can observe a lot, just by looking." Look closely at the wood and notice the direction of its lines and texture—the grain. If the grain is vertical, dust vertically. If the grain is horizontal, dust horizontally.

Regular polishing will nourish and protect the wood. Use commercially available products such as Guardsman Furniture Polish, which comes in a pump and spray (buy the pump!), lemon oil, or make your own using 1 cup olive oil to $\frac{1}{3}$ cup lemon juice. Another option is to mix 2 teaspoons of mineral oil with 1 teaspoon of lemon oil. Use a clean, dry, lint-free cloth and rub all surfaces thoroughly. When in doubt, check the furniture manufacturer's instructions.

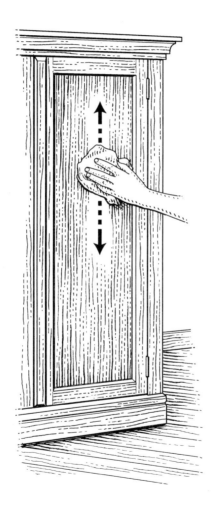

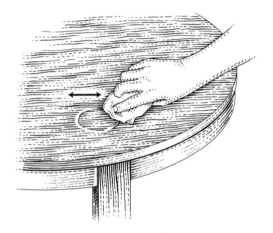

➕ **Rescue:** *Remove hot dish marks by mixing equal parts of boiled linseed oil, available in good hardware stores and home centers, with turpentine. A $\frac{1}{4}$ cup of each should be more than enough. Dampen a soft cloth with the mixture and apply it to the mark. It may take several applications before the stain fades.*

➕ **Rescue:** *Remove water rings with a one-to-one mixture of white vinegar and cooking oil. Dampen a clean cloth with the mixture and rub the ring in the direction of the grain.*

**Painted, Pickled, and Distressed Finishes** Treat painted wood surfaces as you would painted walls, rather than wood. But handle them with more care than you would walls. Dust items thoroughly using a lint-free cloth. After dusting, gently wipe surfaces again with white vinegar using a dry sponge to pick up any remaining dust.

⚠ *Caution:* **Avoid aerosol-based dusting products.**

**4**

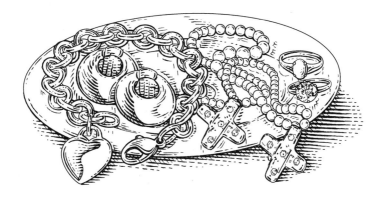

### Jewelry

It's easier than you think to keep all that glitters glittering. Cleaning and preserving your jewels doesn't have to be costly.

⚠ *Caution: Never clean jewelry with loose settings. Take it to a professional and have it repaired, and, at the same time, have it cleaned. Once its settings are firm you can maintain it for years with the following at-home care.*

**Gold** Karat gold can easily be cleaned by soaking in one part ammonia to two parts warm water. (Note: "karat gold" is the jeweler's term for the precious metal, as opposed to the color "gold," used when referring to costume jewelry. This cleaning method is for karat gold only.) Be careful that the jewelry is indeed gold and that any decorative elements that are not gold are covered so as not to be damaged by the

ammonia. If other elements are present, substitute a few drops of mild dishwashing liquid in place of ammonia. After soaking for 15 minutes, gently scrub the item with a very soft toothbrush or makeup brush. Rinse and buff with a clean, soft cloth.

⚠ *Caution: Don't confuse ammonia with chlorine, which will ruin gold.*

**Platinum** Clean platinum using one cup of warm water and $\frac{1}{2}$ cup of ammonia to bring out the precious metal's shine. Soak the item for up to 20 minutes, and then swish in cold water to rinse and place on a tissue to air dry.

**Silver** Simply handling silver jewelry frequently can help maintain its shine, though occasional polishing is necessary to bring out its true brilliance.

For silver that gleams, use silver polish. It can be used often, since it is nonabrasive. Keep a small can of the polish, a soft cloth, a rubber glove, and a toothbrush in plastic bag near your jewelry box for quick polishes before you wear your silver jewelry. Always wash earring studs with water after you polish. Plain white toothpaste works almost as well to clean silver, but it should be used less often as it is abrasive.

Apply silver polish or toothpaste with a soft cloth and work into the silver. Use a soft toothbrush or makeup brush for crevices. With a clean, soft cloth, buff and polish in firm strokes.

Hearth ash is one of the best silver cleaners. It is an extra bonus for those blessed with a working fireplace. Dip a clean, soft cloth in the dry ash and rub vigorously until your piece shines.

**Diamonds and Other Precious Jewels** Like platinum, diamonds can be cleaned effectively using one cup of warm water and $\frac{1}{2}$ cup of ammonia. Soak the stones for up to 20 minutes. Swish in cold water to rinse and place on a tissue to air dry.

⚠ *Caution: This method can be used for many gemstones. However, check with your jeweler first and definitely Do Not use it with emeralds, which are very soft and can be damaged by the solution. Substitute a few drops of mild dishwashing liquid for ammonia and your emeralds will gleam.*

**Costume Jewelry** Avoid exposing costume jewelry—items that are not made of gold, silver, platinum, or precious stones—to household cleaners. The best care is to remove them before doing ordinary household chores.

To clean costume jewelry, sprinkle salt into a glass bowl containing a $\frac{1}{4}$ cup of lemon juice. Soak the item for a few minutes, then rinse in cool water and pat dry. Use a very soft toothbrush, makeup brush, or cotton swab if the piece is heavily worked or detailed.

⚠ *Caution: This method gets great results. However, do not to use it for pearls, real or faux, or foil-backed rhinestones.*

Ethnic or folk jewelry must be cleaned with careful attention to the material from which it is made. Ceramic beads can be cleaned with one cup of warm water and a few drops of dishwashing liquid. Do not submerge the jewelry in water, but dab on the solution with a cotton swab, then follow with a wet cloth to rinse. Do not soak the connecting thread. Use a mixture of one part ammonia to one part water to clean crystal and glass beads.

Often jewelry made from seeds, shells, and other organic materials requires no cleaning. They grow more beautiful with the accumulation of "dirt." Sometimes a swish in the ocean or a pond while you wear them is all they need to get "clean."

Painted Jewelry can be cleaned as other painted surfaces (see page 37). Make sure glue and clasps are sturdy. If clasps are not made of the same material, do not clean them using the same process you use for jewelry itself, or they may be damaged in the cleaning process.

# 5

## Glass, Crystal, and Porcelain

A friend has a collection of small mirrors from many countries. Grouped together and individually, they catch the light wonderfully from the many windows in her living-dining room. That is the beauty of glass. Proper cleaning to maximize the reflective quality of glass can be a challenge. Sometimes it seems that the more we clean it, the more spots and streaks we create. But there is a way to clean glass that is as easy as it is effective.

**Windows and Glass Doors** Straight vinegar and black-and-white newspaper cleans windows best. Use vertical strokes when washing windows on the outside and horizontal inside, so you can tell which side has the streaks. While newspaper works even better than heavy-duty paper towels (and saves money), some people don't like their hands stained black from the newspaper. The stain washes off easily with soap and warm water, but you might want to wear rubber gloves.

Washing windows on a hot, sunny day causes them to dry too quickly and streak.

**Mirrors** Mix two tablespoons of vinegar to $^1/_2$ cup of water and apply to mirrors with a soft, lint-free cloth for mirrors that shine. A soft, lint-free cloth dampened with rubbing alcohol also works wonders.

**Crystal** Clean crystal with care. Avoid anything abrasive. Before washing your crystal by hand, line the sink with paper towels to avoid chipping it, or buy a rubber sink saver that lines the bottom and sides. Warm soapy water is best; very hot water is likely to crack delicate glassware. Bring out crystal's sparkle by adding a few drops of white vinegar to the rinse water. Let your crystal air-dry to avoid the cloudy film towel-drying can cause.

✚ *Rescue: Minimize or eliminate scratches by buffing crystal with white toothpaste and rinsing in warm water.*

**Vases** Keeping vases clean can be a challenge because the residue from plants and water can be very difficult to remove. Treat your vases with care according to the material from which they are made. Wash glass vases on the outside with warm, soapy water and a soft dish cloth.

⚠ *Caution: Never attempt to clean a piece you suspect has been repaired*

To remove cut-flower residue and stains from the inside of glass vases, fill the vase with warm water. Drop in two Alka Seltzer or denture tablets. Let the tablets dissolve completely and after 30 minutes rinse with clear water and let air dry.

If the vase has a fired finish, that is, a shiny glaze—and has not previously been restored—any strong, all-purpose cleaner like Spic & Span will safely clean it. Test an inconspicuous area first using a cotton swab dipped in the cleaner. Rinse immediately. Most bisque, that is, un-glazed porcelain, can also be cleaned using these products, but after cleaning un-glazed finishes, follow with a bleach spray cleaner to remove any dirt left in the tiny pores of the bisque paint. Rinse immediately. Never use a bleach spray cleaner first, as it may set a stain. Only use the bleach spray after the all-purpose cleaner has been completely rinsed off. Fine porcelain that has previously been restored should be cleaned only with a mild dish cleaning detergent. Never soak these items or scrub them with abrasive materials.

Clean all porcelain in a deep sink or tub with an attached hose, if available. Line the sink with towels or a rubber mat so the porcelain does not get chipped.

**6**

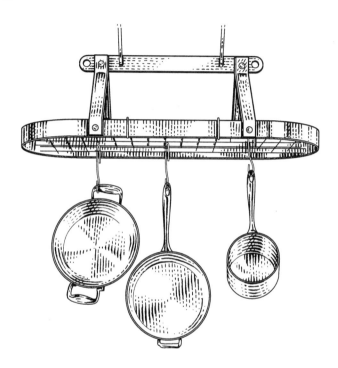

## Metal

The trick to cleaning metal is to keep it bright without scratching the finish. Even with the return to serious cooking and elegant entertaining at home, with today's busy schedules, no one wants to devote time and elbow grease to scrubbing metal cookware and accessories.

**Kitchen Cookware** Aluminum, copper, and nonstick pans are easily cleaned with products found around the house. For aluminum, fill pots or pans with water and add two teaspoons of baking soda or cream of tartar. Place on a back burner, bring to a slow boil and simmer for two to five minutes. Carefully empty water in the sink and allow the pot to cool. Wash with regular dishwashing liquid and a sprinkle of salt. Combine a capful of vinegar and two tablespoons of baking soda in a bowl and stir in two teaspoons of warm

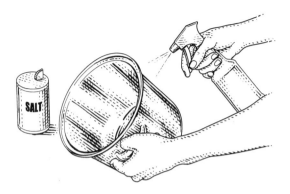

water to make a paste that will clean tough stains in nonstick cookware. Scrub vigorously with a cleaning pad made for nonstick surfaces, and then rinse with warm water.

Clean copper pots with a homemade spray of two cups vinegar and three tablespoons of salt, shaken well. Spray freely on the pot's surface, let stand for 30 minutes and rub clean with your regular dishcloth.

Anodized aluminum is best cared for using the manufacturer's cleaners.

Cast iron, once seasoned, requires only a light wash in dish water and rinsing under warm running water. Dry with a damp cloth, or place on warm stove top to dry. Overexposure to water can rust cast iron or ruin its seasoning.

**Wrought Iron** Avoid abrasive household cleaners that can scratch surfaces. Dishwashing liquid works well. Use a clean, soft cloth to wipe and wipe again with a cloth dampened with clean water to rinse. To avoid rust, wipe dry immediately with a clean cloth.

### 7

### Upholstery, Pillows, Curtains, and Drapes

Upholstered furniture should be washed once a year with mild fabric cleaner such as Easy Clean or a similar product that requires no rinsing, and a stiff but not hard brush. Before washing, test an area under the seat cushions to be sure the item is washable with water. If so, vacuum the item. Then pick up the pillows, and using a wooden spoon or your hand, pound the dust out. If not, call a reputable professional.

Following manufacturer's instructions for the detergent, combine it with warm water in a bucket, creating a layer of foam by agitating with a natural bristle brush. Shake the excess water off the brush and apply the foam to the upholstery, a small area at a time. Work the foam into the fibers of the material. After 20 minutes, wipe off foam with a dry towel to absorb excess moisture. Allow upholstery to air dry thoroughly.

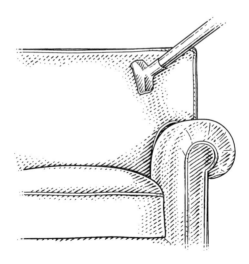

⧗ **Pearl of Preservation:** *Prevent fading by turning cushions over at least once or twice a month.*

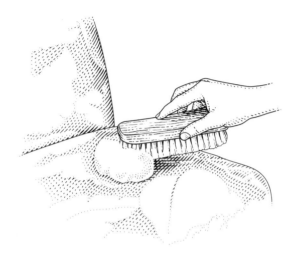

**Pillows** God is in the details: Pillows can be among the most important accents in a home. They can also be magnets for dirt and hair—pet and human. One of the drawbacks to comfortable pillows is that people and pets love to lounge on them, leaving behind dirt, hair, and skin oils. Check the manufacturer's cleaning instructions when you buy pillows.

⧖ **_Pearl of Preservation:_** _Remove the care tag from your new pillow and file it with your other instructions so you will know how to proceed when the time comes._

What pillows are stuffed with and what they are covered in equally determine how they should be cleaned.

Beaded or heavily adorned pillows should always be professionally cleaned. Even if pillows are washable, it is still a good idea to test an inconspicuous area to be sure the color will not fade or run. Pound out the dirt with a wooden spoon. If pillows have removable covers, remove them and follow manufacturer's instructions. If the covers do not come off, wash pillows as you would upholstery, with an upholstery cleaning product, as in previous page, applying suds to the surface only. Regularly spot-clean your pillows to avoid ground-in dirt and keep stains from setting.

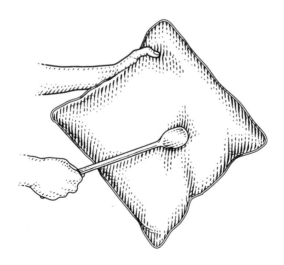

**Down and Feathers** Before cleaning down and feather items check the manufacturer's label. Many are absolutely "dry clean only." If not, wash your down and feather pillows in a top-loading washing machine in warm water and a low-sudsing detergent. Only top-loaders with a 3.2 cubit feet capacity or greater can be used because the machine must be stopped and opened during the wash cycle.

Check that all seams are intact and the fabric is free of rips and tears. If the item is inclined to shed feathers, it will be better in the hands of the dry cleaner.

Place each pillow inside a pillowcase. Set the machine on the gentle cycle, add the laundry detergent and let it dissolve and diffuse before putting in the pillows. Stop the agitation and add the pillows. Feathers are heavy when wet so do not overload the machine.

Halfway through the wash cycle, stop the machine again and turn the pillows over. Run the rinse cycle at least twice—until the water is clear—to make sure all the detergent is rinsed out. To dry, place the pillows in the dryer on low heat for at least 2 hours, along with a sneaker to help fluff the feathers. Add a softener sheet for freshness.

If you have a top-loading washer with a 3.2 cubit feet capacity or greater, you can also wash duvets, one at a time inside a duvet cover, following the steps above.

**Curtains and Drapes** Curtains and drapes should be cleaned regularly—at the change of each season—to eliminate dust and bacteria. Unless labeled "dry clean only," wash in cold water and a mild detergent. Hang them to air dry, or depending on care instructions on the label, use a low setting in the dryer. Remove from dryer immediately to prevent wrinkling.

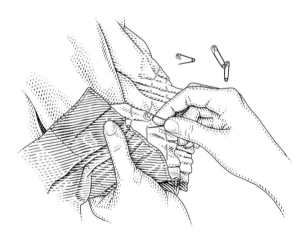

⌛ *Pearl of Preservation: Before laundering, carefully remove hanger attachments that could shred fabric. Place safety pins to mark where hanging devices will be reattached.*

# 8

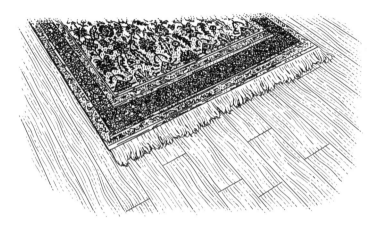

## Rugs and Carpets

The key to preserving rugs and carpets is regular cleaning. Whether they look like they need it or not, floor coverings need to be vacuumed weekly. Dirt weakens rug fibers. Prevent dirt from getting deeply embedded by regular, thorough vacuuming. Go over each area more than once, overlapping your strokes each time.

In the East, flat weave and pile wool and silk Oriental rugs still are cleaned as they have been for centuries. Laid flat out of doors, plain soap and water is applied to them with a brush, followed by clear water to rinse. They are then left in the sun to dry.

Few of us have the space or time for this. Also, new fibers make it necessary to first determine if you can shampoo your rug or carpet, or if it is professional-care only, in which case you will need to send it to the dry cleaner or call in professionals.

Before shampooing rugs or carpet remove all furnishings, or place cardboard under the feet of large items so the permanent imprints are not left on the wet fibers.

Choose a carpet cleaner like Easy Clean. Use one cup of cleaner to one gallon of warm water and agitate with a natural bristle brush. Shake off the excess water from the brush and apply it to the rug, a small area at a time. Work the foam into the fibers. This product requires no rinsing. Vacuum when completely dry.

Spills on your rugs and carpets must be handled quickly. For wine spills, pour on salt immediately, and then blot with a clean towel. Club soda, poured on clean towels also works wonders as a blotter. Avoid saturating the rug. If you are not able to get to it right away, mix $\frac{1}{2}$ teaspoon of Woolite or other fine detergent with 1 cup of cold water. Do not use hot water on stains. Blot the stained area repeatedly with the mixture until the stain lifts. This may take several applications, depending on how long the stain has set. Once the stain lifts, cover it with a towel and press down repeatedly to be sure that the stain removal agents are not absorbed by the rug. Rinse the spot with cold water and blot it with a clean towel. Let it air dry. One part white vinegar to one part water, applied twice with a cloth will usually handle any discoloration that remains.

✛ *Rescue: Pet accidents on carpets can require professional cleaning if not caught right away. If you are able to act quickly, before the urine seeps through to the underpadding, treat the entire area with a nonmasking product like Get the Odor Out.*

**9**

## Linens

Bed linens can determine the atmosphere and comfort of our most personal rooms. One hundred percent cotton, high thread–count sheets (200 and above) can last for decades if well cared for.

⧗ **Pearl of Preservation:** *Always treat stains right away to prevent their setting.*

### ✚ Rescue: The Three Wicked Stains

**Blood:** *Blood that has not set is easy to remove if the stain is kept wet. Rinse the stain under the tap in cold water until it disappears. Launder in cold water. For stains that have set, begin with a prolonged soak in cold water—for several hours—with frequent hand-rubbing on the stain. Rinse and soak again in water with a few drops of ammonia. Launder in cold water. Avoid heat until the stain is completely out; heat will set the stain.*

**Grease from hair, gel, or ointments:** *Treat these stains as quickly as possible as they attract more dirt that can destroy fabric. Blot as much as possible with a paper towel while stain is fresh. Next, remove item from the bed and place stain face-down on clean, white towel. Cover grease spot with baking soda; work the baking soda into fibers and let it sit for one hour. Scrub with a stiff brush and repeat if necessary. Launder as usual.*

**Lipstick/makeup:** *If it is lipstick, scrape off as much as possible, then treat with a prewash, nonaerosol product and rub it with a clean white towel until the stain is gone. Nonaerosol hairspray also works well in place of the prewash. Launder as usual.*

Frequency for washing linens is a matter of personal taste. Some change bed linens weekly, some biweekly, some daily. Table linens may be reused for the better part of a week or changed with each meal. Choose what suits your lifestyle.

For your regular wash, use warm water and the gentle cycle. A tablespoon of Epsom salt per gallon of rinse water will keep colors from running or fading.

Unless you have the luxury of drying your clothes outside in the sun (the best color brightener there is) tumble dry fine linens on low heat. It will take a bit longer, but it is worth it. Remove from the dryer as soon as the spin ceases and fold immediately. Few linens need ironing these days, but if you choose to do so, iron on low to medium heat.

**⧗ Pearl of Preservation:** *Save empty fragrance bottles and place them uncapped in your linen closet (and lingerie drawers) to give your sheets and towels your special scent.*

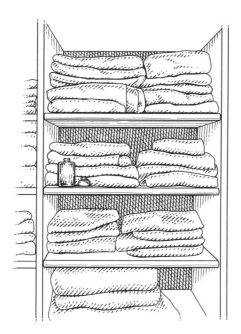

**✛ Rescue:** *Pour table salt on wine spills on table linens— immediately. Let the salt absorb the stain and rinse with cool water. If you cannot immediately remove the tablecloth, pour on the salt and let it sit until the party is over. Then rinse.*

# 10

## Computers and Electronics

Electronics are among the boons of modern life. But they also are one more thing for busy people to have to clean—and carefully. Computers and electronics are composed of high impact plastics, metals, and an array of inner workings that do not fare well when wet. It is essential to use the correct products and procedure to keep your high tech implements running smoothly.

The first step to cleaning your computer is to turn it off. The second is to have the right cleaning products.

**Monitor screen:** With a clean, lint-free cloth dampened with ammonia, wipe the monitor from top to bottom. For regular up-keep between real cleanings, there are now microfiber wipes on the market similar to those used for cleaning spectacles.

**Mouse attachment with a ball:** Remove the ball and inspect it for dirt and dust. Use a cotton swab dampened with rubbing alcohol to clean the ball and its cradle, then replace them.

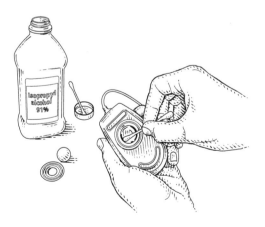

**Keyboard:** First check the manufacturer's instructions and follow any specific instructions. Otherwise, start by shutting down your computer and disconnecting the keyboard. Gently but firmly shake any loose dust from the keyboard. Clean imbedded dirt and dust between the keys using a compressed air appliance, now commonly available at bed and bath stores, or a blow dryer set on cool. Next, dampen a clean cloth with a product specifically designed to clean electronics, like 3M™ Keyboard & Screen Cleaner made by Planna Technology, and wipe the keyboard chassis and the keys. Be sure the cleaning product has fully evaporated before reconnecting the keyboard and starting the computer.

**Fax, Scanner, Photocopier:** Check the manufacturer's instructions. Unplug it. Dampen a clean lint-free cloth with ammonia and wipe the scanner screen. Immediately wipe again using a fresh dry cloth. Clean the body with a commercial product designed to clean plastic or simply use a cloth dampened—not wet—with ammonia.

**CD player, VCR, DVD, or Cassette Player:** Keep these in optimal working order by cleaning the inner workings on a regular basis using head cleaners designed for each and available at electronics stores like Radio Shack. Keep the exteriors clean by dusting with a microfiber cloth on a regular basis. These cloths are great for CDs and DVDs too.

✚ *Rescue: If your electronic equipment gets wet, unplug it immediately. Do not turn it on until it has completely dried out; that may take weeks. Of course, seek technical repair as soon as possible, but under no circumstances turn the machine on until it is completely dry.*

⧗ *Pearl of Preservation: Head- and ear-phones need regular cleaning with a cloth dampened—not wet—with rubbing alcohol.*

## 11

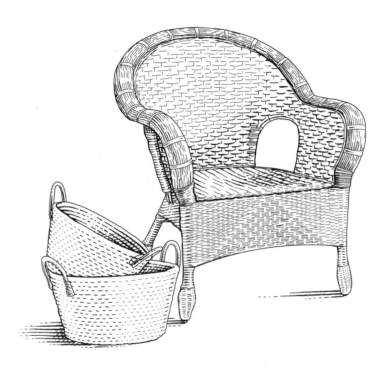

### Wicker and Bamboo

Graceful lines and light silhouettes characterize many wicker and bamboo furnishings. They can evoke a feeling of faraway places or homey comfort. And they are not as difficult to clean as they might seem.

First, loosen dirt with compressed air or a blow dryer set on cool. Rub furniture with a stiff bristle brush dipped in 1 cup of water mixed with $\frac{1}{4}$ cup of table salt. Shake off excess water and brush in the direction of the most prominent weaving or wrapping pattern. Avoid soaking the item unless it is tightly wrapped or it will buckle or unravel. Air dry.

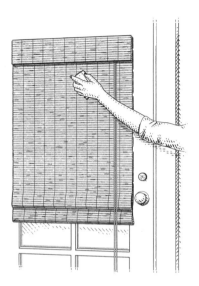

Bamboo blinds can easily be cleaned by dampening—
again, not wetting—a sponge with soapy water and rubbing
widthwise. Blinds may remain hung or be placed in an empty
bathtub. In either case, hang them up to air dry.

**12**

## Dust Collectors

**Picture Frames** To clean painted frames and avoid water that can splatter and damage paint, mix 1 egg white with 1 teaspoon of baking soda. Sponge the mixture on to the frame using a clean, soft sponge. Wipe it off immediately using a clean, slightly damp cloth. Clean gilded frames using a soft toothbrush dipped in the egg white/baking soda mixture. Use a second, clean toothbrush to wipe off the mixture and finish by buffing with a clean cloth.

Tarnished brass or silver frames are easily restored to gleaming beauty by rubbing on turpentine with a soft cloth.

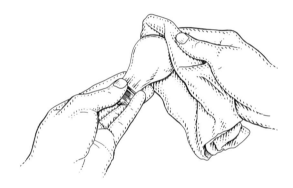

**Lamps** Keeping lamps, shades, and bulbs dirt and dust free contributes to the beauty of the light and is energy efficient. Clean bulbs yield more light.

Disconnect the lamp and allow the bulb to cool. Unscrew cool bulbs from the fixture. With a clean cloth dampened with warm water then squeezed as dry as possible, wipe only the glass portion of the dirty bulb.

Clean lamp bases and shades according to instructions for the material from which they are made. Most fabric

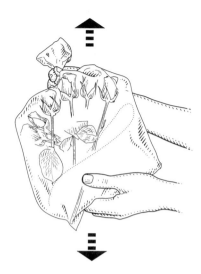

shades, including silk and linen, can be cleaned with a feather duster and, if necessary, a damp cloth. Wipe the shade gently to avoid rings or streaks. Regular dusting is the best solution for preventing heavy dirt buildup. Dust pleated shades using a blow dryer on its coolest setting.

**Dried and Silk Flowers** To clean dried and silk flowers, fill a paper or plastic bag half full of table salt. Add the flowers and hold bag tight or secure with a rubber band. Shake vigorously. The salt will attract the dust, leaving the flowers clean and fresh.

**Fans** All ceiling fan paddles need is regular dusting with a dust-mop style brush and an occasional rub with a cloth or sponge. If the paddles are wood, use Murphy's Oil Soap. White vinegar works wonders on painted surfaces.

# Caring for your possessions can be both rewarding, and cost saving

**But the wisest do-it-yourselfers know when to give place to the pros. To call or not to call can be one of the most important decisions you make regarding your possessions. Here are three cardinal rules, which, along with common sense, should help you make the right call.**

*A hearty laugh gives one a drycleaning,*
*while a good cry is a wet wash.*

PUZANT KEVORK THOMAJAN

**Rule number one:** Follow the manufacturer's instructions. If the tag reads "dry clean only," do so.

**Rule number two:** A stain that has set too long, be it on garment, furniture, or floor, is best put into the hands of a professional.

**Rule number three:** If the item does not say "dry clean only" but a test of a small area shows it is not colorfast, take it to a professional.

# Environmentally Sound Products

*Better keep yourself clean and bright;*
*you are the window through which you must see the world.*

GEORGE BERNARD SHAW

**Earth Friendly Products** www.ecos.com
Earth-friendly products that have won several responsible-business awards. Products range from general cleaning, kitchen cleaning, bathroom, laundry, paper products, pet products, and industrial products.

**Lifekind Naturally Safer** www.lifekind.com
Website with green products for air and water, baby products, beds and bedding, candles, cleaning, furniture, kitchen and bath, laundry, meditation and yoga, personal care, pet products, and sleepwear. Also features chemical research with a glossary, links, and suggested reading. Educational reading on interesting topics can also be found on website.

**Simple Green** www.simplegreen.com
Household products include non-toxic, biodegradable all-purpose cleaners, a product to clean barbecues and microwaves, and carpet cleaners.

**Sun and Earth** www.sunandearth.com
Dish-washing, all-purpose spray, laundry detergent, fabric softener, glass cleaner.

**Magic American Corporation** www.magicamerican.com

Goo Gone and Magic. Professional-strength formulas which utilize readily biodegradable materials to create effective products that contain no toxins.

**Country Save** www.countrysave.com

Founded in 1977 by Elmer Pearson, inventor of Elmer's Glue, Country Save has powdered laundry, non-chlorine bleach, liquid laundry detergent, liquid dish detergent, and all-purpose cleaner. All powder products are 100% Phosphate free, completely Biodegradable and they are fragrance and perfume free and none of the products use dyes or optical brighteners.

**Distinctive Products** www.guardsman.com

Guardsman Furniture Polish.

Available at many national chains.

**Easy Clean** EZ-Clean Co., 2565 Broadway, New York, NY 10025

(718) 583-4084

EZ Clean

**Clarice Taylor** understands the importance of a clean, well-ordered environment. Her work in humanitarian affairs has taken her to some of the most trouble spots on earth. Living in a tent in a Rwandan refugee camp without adequate sanitation and assignments in war torn cities without electricity or water, including Baghdad and Sarajevo, have heightened this understanding and given her a profound appreciation for cleanliness and order in her home—something of a challenge during her years as the single parent of a teenage daughter.

On many occasions in her travels, Clarice has been a guest of people who live in real poverty—some whose homes consist of a dirt floor and baked mud walls. She was fascinated by the care taken in maintaining such humble dwellings—the dirt floor swept in swirling patterns and the walls neatly lined with cooking utensils, the welcome extended regardless of how much or how little there was to share.

Clarice learned the basics of cleaning as a child from her mother, also a working mom. Today, she employs her skills to make a comfortable and hospitable home. Her interest in the home arts includes needlecraft and interior design and she has plans to develop a home decor website, urbanvillagedecor.com. Clarice believes in the intrinsic cultural value of home-as-refuge and believes that creating such an environment is essential in an increasingly hectic world.